# The Music

## Creative, high-interest activities for standards-based music education

## Joy Nelson

## Table of Contents

Alfred

# A Note to the Teacher

*I don't think there is any way possible to have music too early…*
*Music in the lives of the young is probably as important as the*
*breath in their lungs or the blood in their veins. The child who*
*is permitted to brush with music, to cope with it, to dance*
*to it, to feel it, to express it, to make it, is a child who*
*is always several plateaus higher.*

Virgil Fox

Music making is an undeniable part of our lives—a fundamental part of virtually every celebration and event. The true joy of music making is reflected in the communal experience, in sensing the rhythm, in being at ease with one's singing voice, and in playing and moving without care or inhibition. Adults who have grown up without music making often express regret and a sense of loss or yearning for the musical experience that others seem to enjoy so richly and freely.

Today, music is recognized as an important and essential part of a complete education. A unique approach to thinking and learning, music is a powerful tool in the development of imagination, creativity, discipline, concentration, and critical thinking skills. Participation in musical activities enriches the spirit and satisfies basic needs for personal expression. Through music, children deepen their understanding and acceptance of themselves and their neighbors throughout the world.

## Scope

*The Music Effect* series is an engaging, ready-to-use resource for teachers who want to lead children toward music literacy and lifelong enjoyment and participation in music. Each book in the series includes a wealth of energizing and imaginative multi-sensory activities. Each book focuses on an increasingly higher level of musical knowledge, skill, and conceptual development.

Chapters in *The Music Effect* begin with the introduction of a set of related musical ideas, or *concept*s. As each chapter progresses, concepts are reinforced through a wide variety of teaching and learning styles and approaches. Chapters conclude with a "How are we Doing?" chart for use in measuring and assessing musical growth and progress.

Books 1 and 2 are designed for a traditional kindergarten music program. Activities range from easy to challenging and can be readily adapted for use with other groups of primary age children.

## Special Features

Several special features form an important part of *The Music Effect* series:

- Correlation with the *National Standards for Music Education*
- Sequential skill and concept development
- Multi-sensory teaching and learning approaches
- Step-by-step progress toward musical goals and objectives
- A range of easy to challenging activities
- Creative, compelling, ready-to-use activities
- Simple and effective assessment charts
- Reproducible copy masters
- Connections to speech, language arts, storytelling, visual arts, creative drama, dance, poetry, science, social studies, math, and nature.
- Compact disc of all rhymes, songs, and listening selections.

## Correlation with the National Standards

Published in 1994, the *National Standards for Music Education* provide guidance for what children should know and be able to do in music.[1] The nine content standards are:

1. Singing, alone and with others, a varied repertoire of music.
2. Performing on instruments, alone and with others, a varied repertoire of music.
3. Improvising melodies, variations, and accompaniments.
4. Composing and arranging music within specified guidelines.
5. Reading and notating music.
6. Listening to, analyzing, and describing music.
7. Evaluating music and music performances.
8. Understanding relationships between music, the other arts, and disciplines outside the arts.
9. Understanding music in relation to history and culture.

*The Music Effect* series addresses each of the nine content standards through activities that are developmentally appropriate and appealing to students. Books 1 and 2 engage young children in singing and speech activities (standard 1), body percussion and rhythm instruments (standard 2), developing their own musical ideas (standards 3 and 4), responding to pictures and picture strips (standard 5), moving in response to music (standard 6), evaluating musical choices (standard 7), and making connections between music and history, culture, and other curricular areas (standards 8 and 9). The National Standards are clearly correlated and identified with every activity in *The Music Effect* series.

[1] From *National Standards for Arts Education*. Copyright © 1994 by Music Educators National Conference (MENC). Used by permission. The complete National Arts Standards and additional materials relating to the Standards are available from MENC—The National Association for Music Education, 1806 Robert Fulton Drive, Reston, VA 20191

**Speech Activities**

Action rhymes and finger plays are integrated throughout Books 1 and 2. These lively speech activities encourage children to use their voices in imaginative and expressive ways, and provide a familiar and comfortable way to approach standard 1.

**Songs and Singing Games**

Traditional songs and singing games are an integral part of every chapter. To facilitate work with young children, each song has a small vocal range and simple, repeated words and phrases. As singing skills develop, songs representing the great diversity of musical styles, groups, and cultures within the world can be selected and added to the curriculum.

# Rote Teaching

Initially, songs and rhymes are taught "by rote." In a rote approach, the teacher plays or sings the song several times. Gradually, through repetition and repeated listening, children imitate and "absorb" the words, movements, and melody. They join in as they feel comfortable, and memorize and refine their performance as they go along.

Whenever possible, daily music experiences are optimal for young children. These experiences may vary from spontaneous singing to extended periods of planned music activity. Much is accomplished at this age level through imitation of the teacher.

# Swinging the Rhythm

Occasionally, the words "swing the rhythm" appear above the words of a song. The rhythmic "swinging" style can be heard on the accompanying CD.

### Recordings/Compact Disc

A CD is included with each book in the series. The recorded tracks feature traditional folk music, classical music, and rhymes.

### Body Percussion

Body percussion is a frequent approach to standard 2, performance with a musical instrument. Body percussion engages children in patting, snapping, stamping, clapping, tapping, and exploring the sound potential of their own bodies.

### Rhythm Instruments

Suggestions for use of rhythm instruments are included throughout Books 1 and 2. A good basic collection includes instruments representing *metal sounds* (jingle bells), *shaking sounds* (shakers, maracas), *scraping sounds* (sand blocks, guiro), *drum sounds* (hand drums), and *wood sounds* (rhythm sticks, wood blocks).

Ideally, the collection includes a shaker, a set of rhythm sticks, and a jingle bell for each child, and one or more of the other instruments. However, the quality of the sound is more important than the number of instruments available for use. If budgets are limited, teachers are encouraged to purchase high-quality, durable instruments that have a clear and pleasing sound.

### Composing, Arranging, and Improvising

Standards 3 and 4 are addressed through composing, arranging, and improvising activities. Beginning with movement and body percussion, children investigate the sounds and percussive possibilities of their bodies and the space around them. They walk, run, jump, hop, stretch, and twist. They explore high and low, soft and loud, and fast and slow sounds and movements.

Discussion topics and question ideas are included with each activity: "Let's try a different sound. Can you think of another way to play this instrument? Which sound do you like better? Why?" As children make choices, they begin to develop deep conceptual understanding and critical thinking and evaluating skills.

# Reproducible Copy Masters

Reproducible black-line copy masters accompany each book in the series. These visual and tactile aids are coordinated with activities in the chapters, and provide a wonderful ready-to-use resource for meeting standard 5, reading and writing music.

## Listening Activities

Selected listening activities invite children to move in response to recorded music. Multiple teaching ideas and suggestions encourage young learners to explore the music in engaging and varied ways. As listening skills develop, music representing the great diversity of musical styles, groups, and cultures within the world can be selected and added to the curriculum.

## Integrated Learning

Integrated learning is featured throughout Books 1 and 2. Relating concepts in music to other areas of the curriculum, young learners investigate connections between music, drawing, painting, poetry, literature, and movement. They explore form and expression through geometric shapes, visual art, and creative drama. They experience rhythm and melody through storytelling, language, dance, science, and nature.

Gradually, children are introduced to music created by people in different places and historical periods. They are encouraged to consider the value of music and the role of music and musicians in their community and the world.

## Multiple Teaching Approaches

Based on the research of Howard Gardner (United States, b. 1943), *The Music Effect* utilizes five basic teaching approaches designed to facilitate concept development and complement individual learning styles. The five approaches are identified by the following symbols:

 Storytelling

 Kinesthetic

 Visual

 Mathematical/critical thinking

 Creative/related arts

*The Music Effect* introduces new learning through each of the five approaches. Children experience stories and creative drama (*storytelling approaches*), active hands-on music making (*kinesthetic approaches*), pictures and visual imagery (*visual approaches*), exploration of "how" and "why" (*mathematical/ critical thinking approaches*), and activities connecting music with other areas of the curriculum (*creative/related arts approaches*).

## Conceptual Development

Each chapter begins with the introduction of a basic set of musical ideas or *concepts*. These concepts are interrelated and develop slowly and gradually. Since deep and enduring conceptual understanding is based on repetition and a variety of successful experiences, suggestions for reinforcement of each concept are highlighted throughout Books 1 and 2.

## Planning for the Year

The following chart suggests a possible timeline for introducing concepts in a typical kindergarten classroom. The unshaded portion of the chart represents the conceptual learning introduced in Book 1. The shaded portion represents the learning in Book 2.

This timeline is meant to be flexible. Teachers are encouraged to adapt the plan to reflect (1) the time available for music activities, (2) the frequency of activities, and (3) the needs of the group.

| | Month | New Conceptual Learning |
|---|---|---|
| **BOOK 1** | September | **Chapter 1:**<br>Music may have an underlying beat.<br>The beat is steady.<br><br>**Chapter 2:**<br>Sounds may be soft.<br>Sounds may be loud.<br>Sounds may express thoughts, moods, and feelings. |
| | October | **Chapter 3:**<br>The tempo may be fast.<br>The tempo may be slow.<br><br>**Chapter 4:**<br>A phrase may be a question.<br>A phrase may be an answer.<br>The form of a song or rhyme may be "question and answer." |
| | November/December | **Chapter 5:**<br>Music may have rests. Rests can be expressive. |
| **BOOK 2** | January/February | **Chapter 1:**<br>Sounds may walk. Sounds may run.<br>Sounds may form rhythm patterns.<br>Rhythm patterns may be the same or different. |
| | March | **Chapter 2:**<br>There are many sounds around us.<br>Sounds can be identified and classified.<br>Sounds are expressive.<br><br>**Chapter 3:**<br>Sounds may be high.<br>Sounds may be low.<br>High and low sounds are expressive. |
| | April/May | **Chapter 4:**<br>High and low sounds may form melodic patterns.<br>Melodic patterns may be the same or different. |

## Charting Musical Growth and Progress

Each activity in *The Music Effect* includes a musical objective, or *focus.* This focus reflects the primary musical learning that is introduced or reinforced during the activity.

Each chapter includes a "How Are We Doing" page for use in planning and assessment. Organized by standards and musical objectives, this page can be used to document growth and progress as children enjoy and participate in chapter activities.

In conclusion, it is important to remember that active music making is a rich and rewarding aesthetic experience for the teacher and the child. Lifelong enjoyment and participation is the ultimate goal. It is "OK" if young learners are not ready for successful participation and assessment in all activities and concept areas. With time, patience, and experience, they will be ready at another time.

*If I were not a physicist, I would probably be a musician.*
*I often think in music. I live my daydreams in music.*
*I see my life in terms of music. I get most joy in life out of music.*

Albert Einstein, 1929

# Chapter 1: The Steady Beat

Throughout the world, people sing, move, listen and respond to music. Everywhere, young people rock or sway to the beat of a drum, tap their fingers to the steady pulse of a stereo system, dance to the sound of cymbals or steel drums, or clap and chant in response to a pop concert, a political rally, or a favorite sports event.

Each of these activities requires an ability to *sense* or respond to a steady pulse or beat. Though some children acquire skills at an early age, most children need frequent and regular opportunities to develop skills in sensing and responding to an underlying beat.

The activities in Chapter 1 invite young learners to listen and move to a steady beat. From an experiential perspective, children speak, sing, move, dance, play instruments, and create and improvise steady sounds and movements. From a conceptual perspective, they discover that:

*Music may have an underlying beat.*
*The beat is steady.*

## Johnny Taps the Beat

Johnny loved his father's workshop. Every day, he went to the workshop and watched his father paint and saw and pound nails with a steady, even beat *(tap knee steadily)*. More than anything, Johnny wanted to use the hammer and nails. "May I use the hammer?" Johnny asked, hopefully. "Yes," said his dad, "but only when you can tap a steady beat." "Oh," said Johnny, and he started to practice.

Johnny held up his fist and began to tap on his knee. Tap, tap, tap - Thump! The hammer slid off the nail and hit the table. Johnny tried again. Tap, tap, tap – thump! Finally, Johnny held the hammer and tapped with a smooth, steady beat *(tap knee steadily)*.

**Track 1** ## Johnny Works With One Hammer

Traditional

John - ny works with one ham - mer, one ham - mer, one ham - mer.

John - ny works with one ham - mer, then he works with two.

| *Verses* | *Movement* |
|---|---|
| Verse 1: Johnny works with one hammer | Pat one fist on knee. |
| Verse 2: Johnny works with two hammers | Pat both fists on knee. |
| Verse 3: Johnny works with three hammers | Pat fists and tap foot. |
| Verse 4: Johnny works with four hammers | Pat and tap both feet. |
| Verse 5: Johnny works with five hammers | Pat, tap, and nod head. |
| Then he goes to sleep! | Pretend to go to sleep. |

## Listen to a Story

**Focus**    *Listen and move to show a steady beat (standard 6).*

- Read "Johnny Taps the Beat."
- Say: "In music, we say Johnny can tap a steady beat. Can you tap a steady beat with me?"
- Demonstrate a steady hammering movement with one fist on your knee.
- Gradually, add more "hammers" (both fists, a foot, both feet, head).

## Learn a New Song

**Focus**    *Sing and move to show a steady beat (standards 1 and 6).*

**Track 1**

- Say: "Let's pretend to be Johnny in the workshop."
- Sing the song or play the recording of "Johnny Works with One Hammer." Demonstrate the movement.
- Say: "Listen and join in when you are ready."
- Encourage the children to tap their knees and join in singing as they become familiar with the song.
- In future lessons, review the song, gradually inviting children to sing and move independently (without your help).

## Identify Steady Movements

**Focus**    *Identify activities that have a steady beat (standard 8).*

*Describe movements as "steady" or "not steady" (standard 7).*

- Review "Johnny Works with One Hammer."
- Say: "What else could we do in the workshop?" "Can you think of a job that has a steady beat?" (saw a board, paint the wall, mop the floor, sweep the floor, sand the wood, sort the nails)
- Explore and perform each suggestion.
- Ask: "Are these movements 'steady' or 'not steady'?" "Why do you think so?"

## Play a Copycat Game

**Focus**    *Listen and move to show a steady beat (standard 6).*

**Materials**    *A favorite recording with a strong underlying beat (e.g., music intended for moving, marching, dancing, exercise)*

- Say: "Watch what my hands do. Be a copycat." or "Watch and copy me" or "Be my mirror."
- Play the recording.
- As the music plays, model simple steady movements.
- Initially, perform each movement *at least eight times* before moving on to a new movement.
- Begin with simple symmetrical movements performed with both hands (e.g., touch head, touch shoulders, touch knees, pat chest, touch waist, pat chin, pat ears).

# The Grandfather Clock

There is a wonderful grandfather clock in the workshop. This clock is taller than Johnny's father—with a giant pendulum that swings steadily back and forth. Johnny likes to **watch and listen** to the steady **tick tock** of the pendulum.

One day, there was an earthquake near the workshop. The ground shook, the chairs rocked, and tools fell off the shelves. When the ground stopped moving, everything was alright—except the clock.

Johnny watched and listened. The sound was not steady. It was jerky and uneven. All night long, Johnny listened to that uneven sound. The next day, his mom called the clock shop. Soon, a technician came to the house. "No problem," she said, and soon the clock was ticking steadily again.

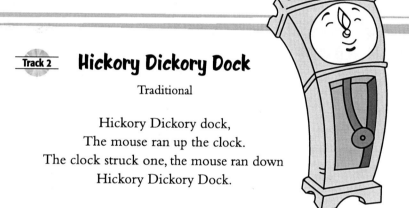

[Track 2] **Hickory Dickory Dock**

Traditional

Hickory Dickory dock,
The mouse ran up the clock.
The clock struck one, the mouse ran down
Hickory Dickory Dock.

## Swing to the Beat

**Focus**    *Identify objects in life that make a steady beat (standard 8).*

*Speak and move to show a steady beat (standards 1 and 6).*

**Materials**   *Copy master 1-A (grandfather clock)*

- Share a picture of a grandfather clock.
- Read "The Grandfather Clock."
[Track 2]
- Ask: "What sounds does the clock make?" "How does the pendulum move?" (steady, swinging movement)
- Say: "Can you say 'tick, tock' and swing your arms with me—like the pendulum of the clock?"
- Say the rhyme "Hickory Dickory Dock" as the children swing their arms.
- Repeat the rhyme and encourage children to join in.

## Identify Steady Sounds

**Focus**    *Identify objects that make a steady beat (standard 8).*

*Describe/evaluate sounds as "steady" or "not steady" (standards 6 and 7).*

- Say: "Can you think of something that makes a steady sound?" (windshield wipers, car turn signal, clock, machine, metronome)
- As items are suggested, make the sounds together.
- Ask: "Is this a steady beat?" "Why do you think so?"

## Read Picture Strips

**Focus**    *Perform a steady beat in response to pictures (standard 5).*

*Choose sounds/movements to show a steady beat (standard 4).*

**Materials**    *Copy master 1-B (clocks)*

- Place four picture strips on the board.
- Ask: "How many clocks (beats) do you see?" "Are these clocks ticking steadily?" "Why do you think so?"
- Say: "Pat your laps and say 'tick, tock' (one sound per picture) as I point to the pictures."
- Ask: "What would you like to do for the last picture?" (e.g., wave your hands, make a ringing sound)

## Play *Picture Strip Mix-up*

**Focus**    *Perform a steady beat in response to pictures (standard 5).*

**Materials**    *Copy master 1-B*

- Say: "Let's play a game. I am going to move the picture strips. Close your eyes!"
- Say: "Open your eyes! Look at the picture strips. Where is the ringing clock?"
- Say: "Let's pat the beat and say 'tick, tock.' Be sure to 'ring' in the right place!"

## Try a Two-Part Challenge

**Focus**    *Speak and move to show a steady beat (standard 1).*

- Divide the children into two groups.
- Ask Group one to swing their arms and whisper "tick, tock."
- Ask Group two to say the words of "Hickory Dickory Dock."
- Signal the "tick tock" group to begin whispering, and then cue the rhyme group to begin speaking.
- If the groups are successful, switch parts.

## Play a Steady Beat

**Focus**   *Choose instruments to play a steady beat (standards 2 and 4).*

**Material**   *Two contrasting instruments or sound makers (e.g., drums and sticks or tone blocks, or pencils and keys).*

- Demonstrate two contrasting instruments.
- Ask: "Which sound makes you think of a clock?" "Which sound do you like best?" "Why?"
- Distribute available instruments.
- Say: "Let's play the beat as we say 'Hickory Dickory Dock.'"

# The Stars and Stripes Forever

John Philip Sousa
(United States, 1855-1932)

When he was a little boy, John Philip Sousa loved music. He loved to go to parades and watch his father march down the street and play trombone in the United States Marine Band. He liked the colorful uniforms, the bright shiny buttons, and the way the musicians marched to the beat (left, right, left, right).

When John Philip Sousa grew up, he became the conductor of the United States Marine Band. He wrote exciting new music that was perfect for marching bands. Everyone loved his music. In fact, he was called the "March King."

## Pretend to be in a Marching Band

**Focus**   *Listen and respond to music intended for marching (standards 6 and 9).*

*Imitate the movements of a drum major (standard 9).*

- Read the story, "John Philip Sousa." (pictures of John Philip Sousa in his band uniform can be viewed on the web site www.dws.org/sousa/pictures.htm)
- Demonstrate marching style (lift knees high, step with the beat).
- Say: "Let's stand and pretend to be in a marching band. Lift your knees and march proudly."
- Ask: "Who would like to be the drum major (marching leader) and 'lead the parade'?"
-  Play "The Stars and Stripes Forever."
- Encourage children to follow the drum major and step with the beat as the music plays.

## Think About John Philip Sousa

**Focus**   *Identify the use and purpose of a march (standard 9).*

- Review the story "John Philip Sousa."
- Ask: "Why was John Philip Sousa called the 'March King'?" "Why did he write marches?"

## Play a *Copycat Game*

**Focus**   *Create movements to show a steady beat (standard 4).*

*Listen and imitate the movements of a drum major (standard 9).*

- Ask: "Can you think of other ways to move to a steady beat?" (pat lap, nod head, touch elbows, rock arms, hammer fists, tap fingers, blink eyes, wiggle toes, pat knees, sway body, flap wings)
- Try the suggested movements together.

- Say: "Let's listen to 'The Stars and Stripes Forever.' I will be the drum major (or beat leader)."
- Model steady movements for the children to "mirror" (copy) as they listen to the music.

## Be a Drum Major

**Focus**   *Improvise steady beat movements (standards 3 and 6).*

*Identify the role of a drum major (standard 9).*

*Listen and imitate the movements of a drum major (standard 9).*

- Ask: "What does a drum major do?" "Can you think of ways the drum major can show a steady beat?"
- "Who would like to be the drum major today?" Choose a child (with good beat sensing skills) to be the drum major.

- Say: "Let's listen to 'The Stars and Stripes Forever' and copy the movements of the drum major. Watch carefully and change when the leader changes!"

## Play an Instrument

**Focus**   *Listen and perform a steady beat in response to pictures (standards 2, 5, and 6).*

**Materials**   *Copy master 1-C (stars and hearts)*

*Two contrasting instruments or sound makers*

- Place two contrasting picture strips on the board.
- Demonstrate two different instruments or sound makers (e.g., sticks and jingle bells, or pencils and keys).

- Say: "Which strip shall we use for the sticks?" "Which strip shall we use for the jingle bells?"
-  Distribute available instruments.
- Say: "Let's listen to 'The Stars and Stripes Forever.' Play your instrument when I point to your picture strip."

## Dancing Lights

**Focus** *Identify objects that make a steady beat (standard 8).*

*Listen and evaluate movements as "steady" or "not steady" (standard 7).*

**Materials** *Flashlight*

- Ask: "Can you think of something that makes a steady flash or blink?" (answering machine, warning light, robot, lighthouse, some tools, some shoes)
- Hold up a flashlight and point it toward the ceiling or wall.
- Ask: "Do you think this (item) can make a steady beat?" "How can we make this light move to show a steady beat?" "Can you think of another way?"
- Invite children to lie down on their backs. Darken the room.
-  Play "The Stars and Stripes Forever."
- Move the flashlight to reflect (dance) a steady beat on the ceiling.

# The Washing Machine Surprise

Jeremy is a good listener. He likes sounds. He likes bugs and animals that make sounds. Sometimes, he brings frogs home and listens to them make croaking sounds, "croak, croak, croak, croak."

One day, Jeremy put his dirty shirt in the washing machine. The shirt swished steadily in the sudsy water, "swish, swish, swish, swish." He put his shoes in the machine, and they bounced to the beat, "bloop, bloop, bloop, bloop." Finally, Jeremy put his jacket in the machine.

Suddenly, "croak, croak, croak, croak!" What was that? Was that his frog?

Yes!

Quickly, Jeremy and his dad rescued the squishy, wet frog from the washing machine. "I'm so sorry," said Jeremy. "I promise I won't do that again." From then on, Jeremy listened to the shirts "swish, swish, swish, swish" and the shoes "bloop, bloop, bloop, bloop"—but he never heard "croak, croak, croak, croak" in the washing machine again.

## Add Sounds to a Story

**Focus**    *Create steady movements/body percussion (standard 4).*

- Read "The Washing Machine Surprise."
- Ask: "What sounds did you hear in the story?"
- Make each of the sounds together.
- Choose a movement/body percussion for each of the sounds.
- Say: "Let's listen to the story. This time, it's your turn to make the sounds."
- Read the story, allowing time for the children to respond.

## Add Instruments

**Focus**    *Choose instruments to play steady sounds (standards 2 and 4).*

**Materials**    *Three contrasting instruments or sound makers (e.g., shaker, drum, sticks, trash can).*

- Demonstrate three different instruments or sound makers.
- Ask: "Which instruments shall we use for the sounds?"
- Assist the children in making appropriate choices: "Which instrument is better for the swishing sound?" "Why do you think so?" "Let's try another instrument." "What would happen if we tried this sound?"
- Distribute the instruments.
- Read "The Washing Machine Surprise," pausing for children to play the instruments.

## Dramatize the Story

**Focus**    *Improvise movements/action for a story (standards 3 and 8).*

- Ask: "What happened in the story?" (Jeremy put the shirt in the machine; the machine made swishing sounds; Jeremy put the shoes in the machine, etc.)
- Encourage children to recall and demonstrate the actions.
- Say: "Let's act out the story."
- Read the story and allow time for the group to improvise actions.
- After the group activity, invite volunteers to play the parts (e.g., Jeremy, the washing machine, the shirt, the shoes, the frog, the dad).
- Read the story and encourage the players to act out their parts.

## Create an Original Steady Beat Story

**Focus**    *Create a story that involves a steady beat (standards 4 and 8).*

- Discuss objects that make a steady sound or blink (e.g., a pair of shoes, windshield wipers, a clock, a robot).
- As a group, choose one of the suggested objects.
- Plan a sequence of events that might happen to/with the object.
- Add sounds and act out the story.

# Let's Review!

As the year progresses, continue to practice and reinforce steady beat.

### Ideas

1. Incorporate steady beat activities as new songs and rhymes are introduced.

2. Continue to review steady beat activities with favorite rhymes, songs, and recordings.

3. Provide frequent opportunities for children to be beat leaders.

### Reminder

Skills and conceptual understanding
develop slowly and gradually,
with time, patience, experience, and practice.

# How Are We Doing?

## Steady beat

Are individuals able to:

1. *sing, alone and with others, a varied repertoire*

    ____speak and move to show a steady beat

    ____sing and move to show a steady beat

2. *perform, alone and with others, on instruments*

    ____perform a steady beat with body percussion

    ____perform a steady beat with instruments/sound makers

3. *improvise*

    ____improvise steady sounds or movements

4. *compose and arrange*

    ____choose or create movements/body percussion to show a steady beat

    ____choose or create sounds to represent a steady beat

    ____choose instruments to play a steady beat

5. *read and notate*

    ____perform a steady beat in response to pictures/icons

6. *listen to, analyze and describe music*

    ____listen and move to show a steady beat

    ____describe sounds or movements as "steady" or "not steady"

7. *evaluate music and music performances*

    ____evaluate sounds or movements as "steady" or "not steady"

8. *understand relationships between music and other arts and disciplines*

    ____identify objects/activities in life that make/have a steady beat
    (social studies)

    ____dramatize (act out) a story  (creative drama)

    ____create/develop a story (language/literature)

9. *understand music in relation to history and culture*

    ____identify the use and purpose of a march

    ____listen and respond to music intended for marching

    ____identify the role of a drum major

    ____imitate the movements of a drum major

## Additional Activities

### Hickety Tickety Bumble Bee  Track 4

Traditional

Hick - e - ty tick - e - ty bum - ble bee, Can you sing your name to me?

**Game Formation**

Children sit in a circle.

**Action**

Players pat a steady beat on the floor as they sing the song. When the song ends, the first player sings his/her name. The group repeats the name. The game continues until each player has had a turn to sing.

### Old MacDonald Track 5

Traditional

Old Mac-Don-ald had a farm E - I - E - I - O! And

on that farm he had some chicks, E - I - E - I - O! With a

chick, chick here, and a chick, chick there, here a chick, there a chick, ev-'ry-where a chick, chick.

Old Mac-Don-ald had a farm E - I - E - I - O!

Verse 2: dog / Verse 3: cow

# Chapter 2: Soft and Loud

Changing the *dynamic level*, or the intensity of the sound, is a powerful means of personal expression. In our daily lives, we clap and cheer when our favorite team scores a point. We whisper softly when we share a secret. We laugh out loud when we hear a joke. Through variations in sound and body movement, we express a variety of thoughts, moods, and feelings.

The activities in Chapter 2 invite young learners to express themselves through changes in the *dynamic level,* or the *loudness and softness* of sounds. From an experiential perspective, children chant, sing, move, play games, explore body percussion, and create loud and soft sounds. From a conceptual perspective, they discover that:

*Sounds may be soft.*
*Sounds may be loud.*
*Sounds may express thoughts, moods, and feelings.*

## Hush Little Baby

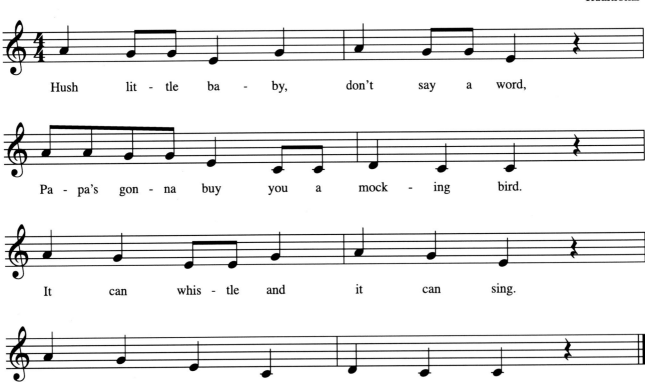

Traditional

Hush lit - tle ba - by, don't say a word,

Pa - pa's gon - na buy you a mock - ing bird.

It can whis - tle and it can sing.

It can do most an - y - thing.

### Listen to the Words

**Focus**  *Relate the words of a song to nature/life experiences (standard 8).*

**Materials**  *Copy master 2-A (mockingbird)*

- Show a picture of a mockingbird.
- Discuss: "What do you know about mockingbirds?" "Mockingbirds live in the southern part of the United States. They can sing many different songs, but can also copy the songs and sounds of many other birds."
- Say: "This song is from Appalachia, in the southern part of the United States. Listen to the words. What can the mockingbird do in this song?"
-  Sing or play the recording of "Hush Little Baby."

### Sing a Lullaby

**Focus**  *Sing and move to show a soft dynamic level (standards 1 and 6).*

*Create "soft" movements (standard 4).*

*Identify the use and purpose of a lullaby (standard 9).*

**Materials**  *Soft stuffed animal or puppet*

-  Sing or play the recording of "Hush Little Baby."
- Rock a soft, fuzzy puppet in your arms as you sing.
- Say: "The puppet is tired and sleepy." "Let's sing the puppet to sleep." "How shall we sing?" (softly, quietly)
- Sing the song and rock or sway. Invite children to join in singing and moving.
- Say: "This song is called a 'lullaby.'" "When would we use a lullaby?" "Why is it important to sing softly?"
- Ask: "Who can think of another 'soft' movement?" (tap shoulders, snap fingers, rub hands, wave arms)
- Say: "Let's sing the song with a different movement." "How shall we move this time?"

### Play an *Echo Game*

**Focus**  *Perform soft and loud sounds with body percussion (standard 2).*

- Say: "Do what I do—like the mockingbird."
- Perform a variety of soft sounds (snap fingers, whisper, click tongue, blow air, meow) and loud sounds (dog barking, motorcycle engine, fireworks, lion roaring).
- Allow time for children to imitate each sound.

## Play a *Picture Game*

 **Focus**   *Relate soft and loud sounds to pictures/objects in the environment (standard 8).*

*Improvise soft and loud sounds in response to pictures/icons (standards 3 and 5).*

**Materials**   *Copy masters 2-B-F (sound pictures)*

- Share several "loud" pictures (fireworks, lion, motorcycle, machines operating, dog barking) and "soft" pictures (basket of kittens, microwave oven, quiet lake, snow scene).

- Say: "Let's make the sounds for these pictures."
- Show the pictures, one at a time, encouraging children to make the appropriate sounds.

## Play a *Sorting Game*

 **Focus**   *Improvise soft and loud sounds in response to pictures/icons (standards 3 and 5).*

*Describe sounds as "soft" or "loud" (standard 6).*

**Materials**   *Copy masters 2-B-F*

- Place contrasting pictures on the board.
- Say: "Let's make the sounds for these pictures" or "Let's turn these pictures into sound."
- Guide the children to sort the pictures into loud and soft groups.
- Ask: "Where shall we put this picture?" "Why do you think so?"

## Strum an Autoharp

**Focus**  *Perform soft and loud sounds (standards 1 and 2).*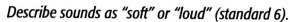

*Describe sounds as "soft" or "loud" (standard 6).*

**Materials**  *Autoharp*

- Press the 'C' chord button and strum the strings on the autoharp.
- Say: "Let's all pretend to strum the strings. 'Strum toward me' or 'strum away from your body'."
- Invite volunteers to try strumming with various items. Try a piece of tag board; a Popsicle stick; a felt covered tongue depressor; a clean rubber door stop; a large plastic paper clip; a felt, metal or plastic guitar pick.
- Ask: "Which makes the loudest sound?" "Which makes the softest sound?" "Which item shall we use for our song?" "Why?"
- Ask: "Who would like to strum the strings while we sing 'Hush Little Baby'?"
- Invite a volunteer to strum the strings while you press the 'C' chord button.

## If You're Happy   Track 7

Verse 2: stomp your feet / Verse 3: shout hurray! / Verse 4: do all three!

## Sing with Body Percussion

**Focus**    *Sing and perform with body percussion (standards 1 and 2).*

 - Sing or play the recording of "If You're Happy."
- Ask: "What sounds do you hear in this song?" (clap hands, stamp feet, shout hooray)
- Sing the song again, encouraging children to join in singing and making the sounds.

*Note: Some children may try to use their outdoor or shouting voices when they sing. If this happens, take time to explore the differences in singing, speaking, whispering, and shouting voices, and the situations that would call for using the various types of voices. Instead of shouting, take a good breath and add energy (intensity) to the voice when speaking or singing loudly.*

## Explore *Found Sounds*

**Focus**    *Create soft and loud sounds using objects in the environment (standards 2, 4, and 8).*

- Ask: "Can you think of a different way to make a loud sound?" "How many different loud sounds can we make?" "How many different soft sounds can we make?"
- Experiment with body percussion sounds and "found sounds" in the room (books, paper, trash cans, pencils, pens).

## Create New Verses

**Focus**    *Sing in a soft dynamic level (standard 1).*

*Create soft sounds (standard 4).*

*Describe sounds as "soft" or "loud" (standard 6).*

- Sing "If You're Happy."
- Ask: "Who can think of a soft sound?" (snap fingers, click tongues, rub hands, whisper hooray, tap heads, etc.)
- Explore the suggested sounds together.
- Ask: "Is this a soft sound?" "Could we make a softer sound?" "How?"
- Sing the song again, incorporating the suggested sounds.

Track 8 **Two Little Sausages**
*Traditional*

| **Words** | **Movement** |
|---|---|
| Two little sausages | Hold thumbs up. |
| Frying in the pan | Wiggle thumbs with the beat. |
| One went "pop" | Pat cheeks during "pop." |
| And the other went "bam." | Clap hands during "bam." |

## Learn a New Rhyme

**Focus**   *Speak and perform the words and movements in "Two Little Sausages" (standard 1).*

- Say: "I have a new rhyme. Listen to the words. What is happening in this rhyme?"
- Say "Two Little Sausages" or play the recording.
- Explore the words and movements together.
- Ask: "Can you hold your thumbs up like this?" "Can you wiggle your thumbs?" "Can you pat your cheeks like this?"
- Repeat the rhyme, slowly and carefully, allowing time for children to say the words and perform the movements with you.

## Explore Different Dynamic Levels

**Focus**   *Choose soft or loud dynamic levels for words in a rhyme (standards 1 and 4).*

*Evaluate choice of dynamic levels (standard 7).*

- Say: "Let's say 'Two Little Sausages' in a loud voice, as if we want everyone to hear."
- Say: "Now, let's say 'Two Little Sausages' in a soft voice, as if telling a secret."
- Guide children to choose dynamic levels for selected words in the rhyme.
- Ask: "How shall we say 'pop'—in a loud or a soft voice?" "How shall we say 'bam'?" "Why do you think so?"
- Say the rhyme together, using a variety of dynamic levels.

## Choose Instruments

**Focus**   *Choose instruments to play soft or loud sounds (standards 2 and 4).*

*Evaluate choice of instruments (standard 7)*

**Materials**   *Three contrasting instruments (e.g., shaker, wood block, drum)*

- Demonstrate three contrasting percussion instruments or sound makers.
- Ask: "Which makes the softest sound?" "Which makes the loudest sound?" "Can this instrument make soft and loud sounds?" "How?" (try tapping or shaking the instrument in different ways).

- Review "Two Little Sausages."
- Ask: "Which instrument shall we use for 'frying'?" "Shall we try another instrument?" "Do you like this sound better?" "Why?"
- Choose instruments for "pop" and "bam."
- Distribute the instruments.
- Say the rhyme together, playing the instruments during the selected words.

# Symphony No. 94 in G Major (Surprise Symphony)

Franz Joseph Haydn
(Austria, 1732-1809)

## The Surprise Symphony

Many years ago, in Eastern Europe, there lived a prince who loved music. Prince Nicholas loved music so much that he hired a famous composer, Franz Joseph Haydn, to write special music for him and his court.

Every night, the musicians played for Prince Nicholas and his friends. Prince Nicholas loved the music, but sometimes his friends would fall asleep in the middle of the concert. So, Mr. Haydn decided to play a joke on his sleeping friends.

"I will write a symphony," he told his musicians, "a symphony that will surprise everyone. But, how can I do that?" "Ah," he thought, "we will play softly—very softly—until everyone falls asleep—and then, the surprise!"

So, the musicians practiced the new symphony. When they were ready, they played the music for the prince and his friends. They played very softly. One by one, the prince and his friends began to fall asleep. Then, suddenly, the surprise! Everyone jumped and opened their eyes. Mr. Haydn laughed happily. It was a great surprise.

Today, you can still hear the music Franz Joseph Haydn wrote for the Prince. It is called the "Surprise Symphony."

## Listen to a Story

**Focus** *Listen and respond to music intended for court life in 18th century Europe (standards 6 and 9).*

**Materials** *Pop-up puppet or finger puppet*

- Read the story "The Surprise Symphony."
- Ask: "What happened to the friends in the story?" "Why did they wake up?" "Can you guess what Mr. Haydn did for the surprise?"
- Hide a finger puppet in your hand, or use a pop-up puppet.
- Say: "My puppet is asleep. Watch and listen. Raise your hand when you see the puppet 'wake up'."
-  Play the "Surprise Symphony" (excerpt). Pop up the puppet when the music becomes louder.

## Dramatize the Story

**Focus** *Dramatize a story (standard 8).*

*Listen and move to show soft and loud sounds (standards 6 and 9).*

- Review the story, "The Surprise Symphony."
- Discuss: "How do you think Prince Nicholas' friends looked (moved) as they were going to sleep?" "Who will show us?" "How did they look when they woke up?"
- Say: "Let's pretend to be Prince Nicholas and his friends." "Pretend to be going to sleep. Wake up or 'act surprised' when you hear the loud sounds."
-  Play the recording of the "Surprise Symphony" (excerpt).

## "Play" a Violin

**Focus** *Listen and move to show loud and soft sounds (standards 2 and 6).*

**Materials** *Copy master 2-G (violin)*

- Share a picture of a violin.
- Say: "Let's pretend that we are musicians for Prince Nicholas. Let's pick up our violins."
- Demonstrate how to hold the (imaginary) instrument in your left hand and the bow in your right hand.
- Say: "This is how we play soft sounds." Demonstrate short, light strokes on the strings.
- Say: "This is how we play loud sounds." Demonstrate longer, more intense movements on the strings.
- Say: "Let's pretend to play our violins for Prince Nicholas."
-  Play the "Surprise Symphony" (excerpt).

## Create Your Own "Surprise Symphony"

**Focus**  *Improvise soft and loud sounds with instruments (standards 2 and 3).*

**Materials**  *Assorted instruments (e.g, jingles, rattles, sticks, drums)*

- Distribute instruments or sound makers.
- Demonstrate/discuss ways to play louder (tap stronger or add more players).
- Demonstrate/discuss ways to play softer (tap softer or use fewer instruments).
- Practice starting and stopping together (watch the teacher's hand cues).
- Say: "Let's create our own 'Surprise Symphony.'"
- Ask: "What shall we do for the surprise?" (play loudly, or play different instruments)
- Ask: "How will we know when to play the surprise?" (watch for a special hand cue, or watch as the teacher points to loud and soft pictures)
- Cue children to begin improvising soft sounds on their instruments.
- Cue the "surprise" and the ending.
- If interest is high, plan a longer performance with more surprises.
- Invite a guest to listen to the "Surprise Symphony."

# Let's Review!

As the year progresses, continue to reinforce soft and loud and steady beat.

### Ideas

1. Explore the expressive use of soft and loud as new songs and rhymes are introduced.
2. Review soft and loud activities with favorite rhymes, songs, and recordings.
3. Provide opportunities to play instruments and move to a steady beat.

# How Are We Doing?

## Soft and Loud

Are individuals able to:

1. *sing, alone and with others, a varied repertoire*

____speak in soft or loud dynamic levels

____sing in soft or loud dynamic levels

2. *perform, alone and with others, on instruments*

____perform soft and loud sounds with body percussion or "found" sounds

____perform soft and loud sounds with instruments or sound makers

3. *improvise*

____improvise soft or loud sounds

4. *compose and arrange*

____choose or create soft or loud sounds or movements

____choose or create instruments/sound makers to play soft or loud sounds

____choose soft or loud dynamic levels to express thoughts, moods, or feelings

5. *read and notate*

____perform soft or loud sounds in response to pictures/icons

6. *listen to, analyze and describe music*

____listen and move to show soft or loud

____describe sounds as "soft" or "loud"

7. *evaluate music and music performances*

____evaluate/justify choices of soft or loud dynamic levels

____evaluate/justify choices of instruments

8. *understand relationships between music and other arts and disciplines*

____relate the words of a song to nature/life experiences (nature, social studies)

____relate soft and loud sounds to pictures/objects in the environment (visual art, nature, social studies, science)

____dramatize (act out) a story (creative drama)

9. *understand music in relation to history and culture*

____identify the use and purpose of a lullaby

____listen and respond to music intended for court life in 18th century Europe

# Additional Activities

## Five Little Pumpkins    Track 10

Traditional Action Rhyme

*Words*

Five little pumpkins sitting on a gate.
The first one said, "Oh my, it's getting late."
The second one said, "There are raindrops in the air."
The third one said, "But we don't care!"
The fourth one said, "Let's run and run and run."
The fifth one said, "I'm ready for some fun."
Then "ooo" went the wind and
"Out" went the light and the
Five little pumpkins rolled out of sight.

*Movement*

Lift hands and show 5 fingers
Cup hands near mouth
Wiggle fingers downward
Cross arms on chest
Roll hands
Place fists on waist
Cup hands near mouth
Clap hands on *out*
Roll hands

## Track 11    Get On Board

Spiritual

Verse

The gos-pel train is com-ing, I hear it close at hand.___ I hear the train wheels roll-ing, and rum-bling through the land. Get on

Refrain

board, lit-tle chil-dren. Get on board, lit-tle chil-dren. Get on board, lit-tle chil-dren. There's room for man-y a more!

Verse 2: The gospel train is coming, I hear it 'round the curve. It's using all its power, and straining every nerve!

Verse 3: The gospel train is coming, the rich and poor are there. No second class aboard this train, no difference in the fare!

# Chapter 3: Tempo

Throughout the day, our hearts beat at different rates of speed. When we think we might be late for a special event, our heart rates quicken and we move at a faster pace. When we are relaxing or walking leisurely with a friend, our heart rate slows down.

Similarly, the beat in music may move at different rates of speed, or different **tempos.** The activities in Chapter 3 invite young learners to experience and explore faster and slower tempos in music. From an experiential perspective, children sing, move, play instruments, create, and play games. From a conceptual perspective, they discover that:

*The tempo may be fast.*
*The tempo may be slow.*

Track 12    **Paige's Train**

Traditional

**Lento (Slow)**

Paig - e's train    goes   so   slow,    takes   so   long to get to   Buf - fa - lo.

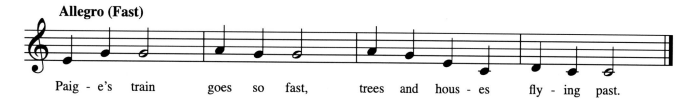

**Allegro (Fast)**

Paig - e's train    goes   so   fast,    trees   and   hous - es    fly - ing   past.

Verse 2: Paige's train climbs a hill, will he make it, yes he will.
Paige's train runs so fine, rockin' and A-Rollin' on down the line.

# A New Tempo for the Train

Once upon a time there was a train that worked in the mountains. The engineer's name was Paige. Every day, Paige's train chugged along the track carrying loads of lumber and coal—always moving at the same speed—always with a slow steady tempo.

One day, Paige got a call. Three hikers were stranded on the mountain. Would Paige be able to rescue them? Paige wasn't sure, but he would certainly try.

Slowly and steadily, Paige moved the train out of the station. He began to sing *(Paige's train goes so slow, takes so long to get to Buffalo)*. Soon, Paige sang faster *(Paige's train goes so fast, trees and houses flying past)*. Then, slowly up the mountain *(Paige's train climbs a hill. Will he make it, yes he will)*.

Suddenly, Paige saw the hikers shouting and waving their arms. Happily, he put them on the train and took them back down the mountain *(Paige's train runs so fine, rockin' and A-Rollin' on down the line)*. Everyone was safe, and Paige was a hero.

To this day, people say that when the train moves slowly, Paige sings in a slow tempo. When the train moves faster, he sings in a fast tempo.

## Respond to a Story

**Focus**   *Relate fast and slow tempos to the speed of a moving train (standard 8).*

*Listen and move to show a fast or slow tempo (standard 6).*

- Read "A New Tempo for the Train."
- Say: "Let's pretend we're on Paige's train. Pat your laps (or slide your hands together) with me."

 **Track 12** · Sing or play the recording of "Paige's Train."

## Do an Elbow Walk

**Focus** *Sing and move to show a fast or slow tempo (standards 1 and 6).*

*Describe a tempo as "fast" or "slow" (standard 6).*

*Identify the use and purpose of fast and slow tempos in music (standard 9).*

- Review the story "A New Tempo for the Train."
- Ask: "How did Paige's train move when it was going up the mountain?" "How did it move when it was going down the mountain?" "Why do you think so?"
- Say: "When the train moved slowly, we say it was moving in a slow tempo." "Let's try 'walking our elbows.'" "Let your elbows move in a slow tempo." "Let your elbows move in a fast tempo."
- **Track 12** • Say: "Let's sing 'Paige's Train' and show the tempos with our elbows."

## Draw a Shape

**Focus** *Relate fast and slow tempos to drawing (standard 8).*

*Improvise movements in a fast or slow tempo (standard 3).*

- Say: "Let's draw in the air." "Let's draw a circle very slowly." "Let's draw circles very quickly."
- Ask: "Which tempo do you like best?" "Why?"
- Try drawing other shapes or letters in different tempos.

## Play Instruments

**Focus** *Sing and play instruments in a fast or slow tempo (standards 1 and 2).*

*Describe a tempo as "fast" or "slow" (standard 6).*

**Materials** *Sticks or sand blocks*

- **Track 12** • Sing "Paige's Train" and play the beat on an instrument.
- Say: "Watch and listen." "How do I play when the train is moving in a slow tempo?" "How do I play when the train is moving in a fast tempo?"
- Say: "Imagine that you are holding a pair of sticks. Let's sing 'Paige's Train' and pretend to play the sticks."
- Distribute available instruments.
- Sing and play the instruments with "Paige's Train."

# Engine, Engine

Traditional Rhyme

Engine, engine Number Nine,
Going down Chicago line.
If the train goes off the track,
Will I get my money back?
Yes, no, maybe so,
Yes, no, maybe so!

## Learn a New Rhyme

**Focus**   *Speak in a fast or slow tempo (standard 1).*

- Say: "Let's pretend to take a ride on a train." "Can you slide your hands together (or pat your lap) like this?"

- Say the rhyme "Engine, Engine" as the children move their hands.
- Say: "Let's try saying the rhyme very slowly." *(Lento)*
- Say: "Let's try it in a walking tempo." *(Andante)*
- Say: "Let's try it in a fast tempo." *(Allegro)*

## Read Picture Strips

**Focus**   *Perform fast or slow in response to pictures (standard 5).*

**Materials**   *Copy master 3-A (trains)*

- Hold up a picture strip.
- Say: "Let's say 'chug' when I point to the pictures."
- Ask: "How would you say the words if the train was going up a mountain?" (slowly) "How would you say the words if the train was going down a mountain?" (fast)
- Try pointing and speaking in different tempos.

### Touch a Picture Strip

**Focus** *Perform fast or slow in response to pictures (standard 5).*

**Materials** *Copy master 3-A*

- Hold up a picture strip.
- Say: "Let's say 'chug' as I point to each picture."
- "Now, point your fingers in the air and say 'chug' as I point to the pictures."
- Ask: "Who would like to touch (point to) the pictures?"
- Invite volunteers to point as the group speaks.

*Note: The child who is pointing is actually "setting" or "controlling" the tempo.*

### Try a Two-Part Challenge

**Focus** *Speak in a fast or slow tempo (standard 1).*

- Divide the children into two groups.
- Ask Group one to whisper "chug, chug."
- Ask Group two to say the rhyme "Engine, Engine."
- Say: "Let's try both groups at the same time."
- Cue Group one to begin whispering, and then cue Group two to begin speaking.
- Repeat the activity using different tempos.

### Create an Introduction

**Focus** *Create an introduction for a rhyme (standards 1 and 4).*

- Say: "Let's imagine the sounds of a train." "What do you hear?"
- Explore sounds together (e.g., the whistle—whoo-oo-oo; the steam escaping by the wheels—shhhhhh; the engine—chug, chug).
- Ask: "What sound does the whistle make? "How could we make that sound?" "What would happen if we tried another sound?" Assist the children in making appropriate choices.
- Select one or more sounds to perform as an ***introduction*** (a beginning, or opening section for the rhyme).
- Perform the sounds as an introduction for the rhyme "Engine, Engine."

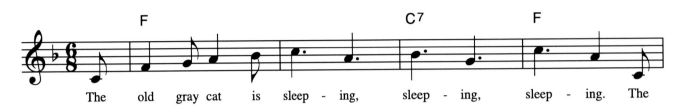 **Track 14** **The Old Gray Cat**

Traditional

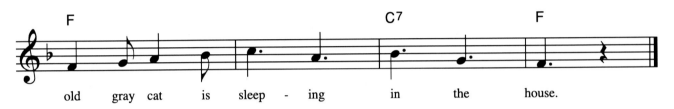

The old gray cat is sleep - ing, sleep - ing, sleep - ing. The

old gray cat is sleep - ing in the house.

**Verses**

Verse 1: The old gray cat is sleeping
Verse 2: The little mice are creeping
Verse 3: The little mice are nibbling
Verse 4: The little mice are crunching
Verse 5: The old gray cat is waking
Verse 6: The little mice are running

**Action**

Lean head on clasped hands
Walk fingers in the air
Pretend to nibble cheese
Pat laps with the beat
Stretch and yawn
Run fingers up and down arms

## Learn a New Song

**Focus**   *Sing verses of a song in fast or slow tempos (standard 1).*

**Track 14**
- Sing or play the recording of "The Old Gray Cat."
- Ask: "What are the little mice doing in the song?" "What is the cat doing?"
- Sing the song again, modeling the movements.
- Encourage children to join in as they become familiar with the song.

## Choose a Tempo

 **Focus**  *Select tempos for verses of a song (standards 1, 4, and 9).*

*Justify/evaluate choice of tempo (standard 7).*

- Guide children to select appropriate tempos for verses 5 and 6 of "The Old Gray Cat."
- Say: "Today, let's decide how we will sing 'The Old Gray Cat.'"
- **Track 14** · Explore: "Let's try singing Verse 6 in a slow tempo." "Let's try singing in a fast tempo." "Which do you like best?" "Why?"
- Ask: "How shall we sing when the cat is waking?" "Why do you think so?"
- Sing the song together using the selected tempos.

## Play the *Cat's Game*

**Focus**  *Sing and move to show a fast or slow tempo (standards 1 and 6).*

### Game Formation

One player is the *cat* and sits with eyes closed in the center of the room. The remaining players pretend to be *mice*. One area of the room is designated as a *safe zone.*

 **Track 14**   ### Action

The *mice* sing the verses, pantomiming the words and moving freely within the space. During *verse 6*, the *mice* run to the *safe zone.* The *cat* attempts to tag *mice* before they reach the *safe zone.* Tagged players become *cats.* The game is repeated until all of the players are *cats* (have been tagged).

# Let's Review!

As the year progresses, continue to reinforce steady beat and tempo.

### Ideas

1. As a new song or rhyme is introduced, encourage children to choose an appropriate tempo.

2. Create steady beat movements for familiar songs and rhymes.

3. Perform a song in different tempos for a special guest or a school program.

# How Are We Doing?

## Tempo

Are individuals able to:

1. *sing, alone and with others, a varied repertoire*

____speak in a fast or slow tempo

____sing in a fast or slow tempo

2. *perform, alone and with others, on instruments*

____play an instrument in a fast or slow tempo

3. *improvise*

____improvise movements in a fast or slow tempo

4. *compose and arrange*

____select a tempo for a song or rhyme

____create an introduction for a song or rhyme

5. *read and notate*

____perform fast or slow in response to pictures/icons

6. *listen to, analyze and describe music*

____listen and move to show a fast or slow tempo

____describe a tempo as "fast" or "slow"

7. *evaluate music and music performances*

____justify/evaluate choices of fast or slow tempos

8. *understand relationships between music and other arts and disciplines*

____relate fast or slow tempos to objects/life experiences (nature, social studies)

____relate fast or slow tempos to drawing (visual arts)

9. *understand music in relation to history and culture*

____identify the use and purpose of fast and slow tempos in music/language

# Chapter 4: Question and Answer Form

Many of us have an innate sense or desire for form and order. We organize our bookshelves, our closets, or our daily appointment books. We tell stories that have a beginning, middle, and end.

In similar ways, musicians use *form* to organize their musical ideas. The form of most children's songs is similar to the way in which *questions and answers* are used in everyday conversation. The first musical thought, or *phrase,* sounds *incomplete,* as if a question has been asked. The second phrase sounds *complete,* as if the question has been answered. Thus, the form of many children's songs and rhymes is *question and answer*, or antecedent and consequent.

Experience with question and answer form provides a firm foundation for understanding and appreciating all forms of musical expression. The activities in Chapter 4 invite young learners to experience and explore question and answer form. From an experiential perspective, the activities invite children to sing, move, explore, read, create, and improvise musical questions and answers. From a conceptual perspective, children discover that:

*A phrase may be a question.*
*A phrase may be an answer.*
*The form of a song or rhyme may be "question and answer."*

### Track 15   Doggie, Doggie

Traditional

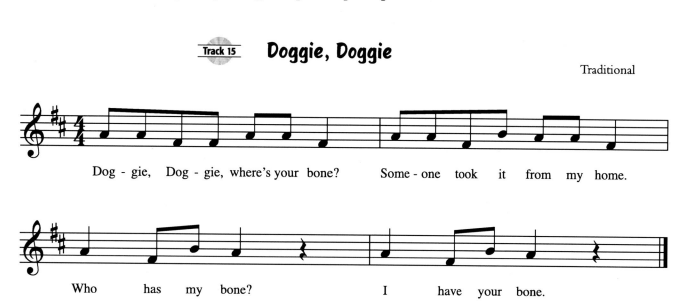

Dog - gie, Dog - gie, where's your bone?     Some - one took it from my home.

Who has my bone?     I have your bone.

## Doggie's Bone

All of the animals on the farm knew *Doggie,* the big black Labrador. They also knew that he had a favorite bone—a bone that he loved. Everyday, they asked the same question, "Doggie, do you have your bone?" and everyday he answered by barking and wagging his tail.

One bright and sunny morning, Doggie could not find his bone. He searched everywhere. What could he do? "Ask your friends," someone said. So, Doggie asked his friends.

"Sally, do you have my bone?" he asked. "No, I do not have your bone," she answered. "Micci, do you have my bone?" "No," she answered, "I do not have your bone." "Ryan, do you have my bone?" "No, he said, "I do not have your bone." "Oh," said Doggie sadly, and he put his head between his paws.

Suddenly, Jenny came running toward him. "Doggie," she said in an excited voice. "I have your bone. I found it in the barn—and here it is." Everyone clapped and cheered, and, once again, Doggie had his bone.

## Listen and Sing

**Focus**    *Relate question and answer phrases to questions and answers in conversation (standard 8).*

*Sing a song in question and answer form (standard 1).*

- Read "Doggie's Bone."
- Ask: "Who remembers Doggie's question?" "Who remembers the answer?"
- Say: "Sometimes, if we listen carefully, we can hear questions and answers in music."
- **Track 15** — Sing or play the recording of "Doggie, Doggie."
- Ask: "What was the question?" "What was the answer?"
- Sing "Doggie, Doggie," encouraging children to join in singing the questions and answers.

## Sing with Pictures

**Focus**  *Sing in response to pictures (standards 1 and 5).*

**Materials**  *Copy masters 4-A and 4-B (two contrasting pictures)*

- Review "Doggie, Doggie" with the children.
- Hold up the first picture while the children sing the question phrases.
- Hold up the second picture while they sing the answer phrases.

*Doggie, Doggie, where's your bone?*
**Someone took it from my home.**
*Who has my bone?*
**I have your bone.**

## Sing in Two Groups

**Focus**  *Sing in response to pictures (standards 1 and 5).*

**Materials**  *Copy masters 4-A and 4-B (two contrasting pictures)*

- Review "Doggie, Doggie."
- Divide children into two groups.
- Ask Group one to sing when you hold up the first picture (the questions).
- Ask Group two to sing when you hold up the second picture (the answers).
- Say: "Sing when I hold up your picture." "Watch and listen when the other group is singing."

## Play *Doggie's Question and Answer Game*

**Focus**   *Sing a song in question and answer form (standard 1).*

**Materials**   *Toy bone*

### Game Formation

Children sit in a circle. One child is chosen to be the *doggie*. A bone is placed near the *doggie*.

While the *doggie's* eyes are closed, another child is chosen to be the *woofer*. The *woofer* quietly takes the *doggie's bone* and hides it behind his/her back. All Children hide their hands behind their backs. The *doggie* opens his/her eyes.

### Action

The group sings, "Doggie, Doggie, where's your bone?" The *doggie* answers, "Someone took it from my home." The *doggie* sings, "Who has my bone?" and the *woofer* answers with a short dog bark (or sings "I have your bone.") The *doggie* has three chances to guess who has the bone. If the doggie guesses incorrectly, the woofer sings "I have your bone." The game begins again with a *new doggie* and a *new woofer.*

 **Track 16**   # Here Is the Bee Hive

England

| *Words* | *Hand Movements* |
|---|---|
| Here is the bee hive, where are the bees? | Make bee hive with hands. |
| Hiding away where nobody sees. | Look inside the bee hive. |
| They are coming out now, they are all alive. | Wiggle fingers upward. |
| One, two, three, four, five! | Count bees with fingers. |
| Bzzzzzzz! | Hide fingers behind back. |

## Learn a New Rhyme

**Focus**   *Listen and move to show question and answer form (standard 6).*

 **Track 16**

- Say: "I have a new rhyme for you. Listen carefully. Do you hear a question?"
- Say the rhyme "Here is the Bee Hive" for the children.
- Ask: "Who remembers the question?" "What was the answer?"
- Model the hand movements, one at a time.
- Say: "Let's make a bee hive." "Look inside your bee hive." "Wiggle your fingers upward." "Count your bees." "Buzz your fingers behind your back."
- Repeat the rhyme, slowly and carefully, allowing time for children to perform the movements.
- In future lessons, review the rhyme, encouraging children to memorize the words and movements.

## Play a *Microphone Game*

**Focus**  *Say a rhyme in question and answer form (standard 1).*

**Materials**  *A toy microphone*

- When children are familiar with "Here is the Bee Hive," divide them into two groups.
- Ask Group one (the question group) to speak when you point the microphone toward them.
- Ask Group two (the answer group) to speak when you point toward them.
- Point the microphone toward each group when it is their turn to speak.
- Say: "Everyone 'bzzzz' at the end!"

## Play an *Improvisation Game*

**Focus**  *Improvise a question or answer (standard 4).*

**Materials**  *A toy microphone or telephone*

- Point the microphone toward yourself as you ask a question, and toward the child as he/she answers.
- Ask: "How are you today?" (I am fine.) "What's your favorite color?" (My favorite color is pink.) "What's your favorite song?" (My favorite song is "Jingle Bells.")
- Encourage children to use complete sentences.
- When everyone is comfortable with speaking questions and answers, try *singing* the questions and answers.

**Track 17**  **All the Little Ducklings**

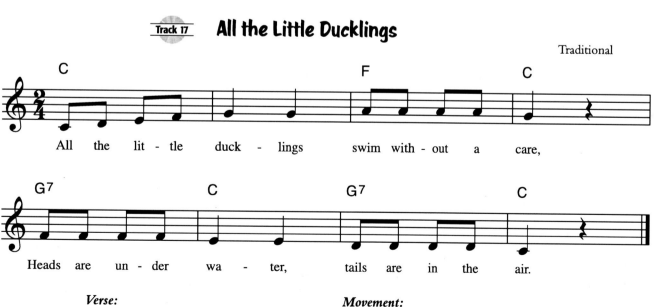

*Verse:*
All the little ducklings
Swim without a care.
Heads are under water,
Tails are in the air.

*Movement:*
Move arms, imitating a
swimming stroke.
Tip head downward.
Shake bottom.

## Learn a New Song

**Focus**　*Sing a song in question and answer form (standard 1).*

*Relate the words of a song to nature/life experiences (standard 8).*

- Ask: "Who can show us a swimming stroke?" "Who can show another stroke?" (back stroke, crawl, dog paddle) "How will our arms move for this stroke?"
- Say: "Try tipping your head down. Try shaking your tail feathers."
- Sing or play the recording of "All the Little Ducklings." Demonstrate the movements.
- Sing the song again, encouraging children to join in singing and moving.

*Note: The words of "All the Little Ducklings" are not conversational questions and answers. From a musical perspective, however, the two phrases are in question and answer form.*

## Sing with Pictures

**Focus**　*Sing in response to pictures representing question and answer form (standards 1 and 5).*

**Materials**　*Copy masters 4-C and 4-D (two contrasting pictures)*

- Review "All the Little Ducklings" with the children.
- Hold up the first picture while the children sing the question phrase.
- Hold up the second picture while they sing the answer phrase.
- Divide into two groups.
- Ask Group one to sing the question and Group two to sing the answer.

*All the little ducklings swim without a care.*　　*Heads are under water, tails are in the air.*

## Add Instruments

**Focus**　*Choose and play instruments in question and answer form (standards 2 and 4).*

*Justify/evaluate choice of instruments (standard 7).*

**Materials**　*Two contrasting percussion instruments*

- When children are familiar with "All the Little Ducklings," demonstrate two contrasting percussion instruments.
- Guide them to choose one instrument for the question and a different instrument for the answer.

- Ask: "Which instrument shall we play during the question phrase?" "Which instrument shall we play during the answer phrase?" "Should we play the same instrument for the question and the answer?" "Why or why not?"
- Distribute the instruments.
- Review: "Who will play during the question phrase?" "Who will play during the answer?"
- Begin singing "All the Little Ducklings," and, if needed, cue children when it is their turn to play.

## Sing With an Illustrated Children's Book

**Focus**   *Relate question and answer phrases to pictures (standard 8).*

- Select an illustrated children's book that features separate pages for each phrase of a poem or song. [1]
- Sing the song as the children look at the pictures.

## "The Wild Horseman"
## Album for the Young

Robert Schumann
(Germany, 1810–1856)

## Robert Schumann

In just a moment, I am going to play some very special music for you. Long ago, in Germany, a composer named Robert Schumann wrote this music as a birthday present for his daughter. He liked to write music for children. Once he wrote a letter to a friend and said that writing music for children made him very happy and put him in a good mood. He said it gave him great joy and happiness.[2]

Robert Schumann's daughter loved horses. This music tells a story about a horse.

Close your eyes and listen to the music. Listen with your imagination. What do you think the horse is doing?

[1] *Suggested Books: All the Pretty Little Horses, illustrated by Linda Saport (New York: Clarion Books); Hush Little Baby, illustrated by Marla Frazee (New York: Harcourt Brace); Brown Bear, Brown Bear, What Do You See? by Bill Martin, Jr., illustrated by Eric Carle (New York: H. Holt and Company).*

[2] *Willard A. Palmer, editor, Album for the Young, Opus 68 by Robert Schumann, published by Alfred Publishing Co., Inc., 1993, p. 2.*

## Listen and Imagine

**Focus**   *Listen and respond to music intended to tell a story (standard 9).*

*Track 18*

- Read the story about Robert Schumann.
- Play the recording of "The Wild Horseman."
- Ask: "Were you able to imagine the horse?" "What did your horse look like?" "What was your horse doing?"

## "Ride" on a Horse

**Focus**   *Listen and move to show question and answer phrases (standard 6).*

*Track 18*

- Say: "Let's imagine we are riding a horse. 'Take hold of the reins' and do what I do."
- Play the recording of "The Wild Horseman."
- Use both hands to draw a "rainbow" in the air during the each question phrase (8 beats).
- Draw another rainbow or a large circle or "sun" during the each answer phrase (8 beats).

## "Ride" over the Hills

**Focus**   *Listen and respond to pictures representing question and answer form (standards 5 and 6).*

**Materials**   *A white board and marker*

*Track 18*

- Draw two hills on the board.
- Say: "Let's imagine a horse galloping over the hills." "Hold up your fingers and do what I do."
- Play the recording of "The Wild Horseman."
- As the children listen, move your fingers (like rabbit ears) up and over the first hill during each question phrase (8 beats).
- Move your fingers up and over the second hill during each answer phrase (8 beats).

## Add Instruments

**Focus** *Play instruments in response to pictures representing question and answer form (standards 2 and 5).*

**Materials** *Shakers and rhythm sticks*

*Copy master 1-C (hearts and stars)*

- Place two picture strips on the board.
- Distribute shakers and rhythm sticks.
- Say: "When I point to the stars, the children with sticks will play (question phrases). When I point to the hearts, the children with shakers will play (answer phrases)."
 - Play "The Wild Horseman" and point to each card twice as the children play.

Question:  Answer:

## Wave Streamers

**Focus** *Listen and wave streamers to show question and answer phrases (standards 6 and 8).*

**Materials** *Colored scarves or streamers (two or more colors)*

- Demonstrate/show the streamers.
- "Which color(s) shall we wave during the question phrases?" "Which color(s) shall we wave during the answer phrases?"
- Distribute the streamers.
 - Play "The Wild Horseman" and guide children to wave their streamers during the appropriate phrases.

## Gallop like Horses

**Focus** *Listen and move to show question and answer phrases (standard 6).*

- Divide the children into two groups.
- Say: "Let's gallop with our fingers in the air."
- "Group one will gallop during the question phrases."
- "Group two will gallop during the answer phrases."
- Play "The Wild Horseman."
- If children are successful with the finger movements, invite them to find a personal space in the room.
 - Play "The Wild Horseman," inviting children to gallop with the phrases.

## Let's Review!

As the year progresses, continue to review question
and answer form, steady beat, and soft and loud.

### Ideas

1. Review your favorite question and answer activities with familiar songs
   (e.g., "Two Little Sausages," page 27, and "Paige's Train", page 33).

2. Discover the question and answer form in new songs and rhymes
   ("Here is the Bee Hive," pages 44, 52; "Baa, Baa, Black Sheep," page 52;
   "Bow Wow Wow," page 53; "Naughty Kitty Cat," page 57)

3. Choose a way to show the beat during the question phrases. Sing softly
   or show the beat in a different way during the answer phrases.

# How Are We Doing?

## Question and Answer Form

Are individuals able to:

1. *sing, alone and with others, a varied repertoire*

_____say a rhyme in question and answer form

_____sing a song in question and answer form

2. *perform, alone and with others, on instruments*

_____play a question or answer phrase with an instrument

3. *improvise*

_____improvise a question or answer phrase

4. *compose and arrange*

_____create movements for a question or answer phrase

_____choose instruments for question or answer phrases

5. *read and notate*

_____respond to pictures/icons representing question and answer form

6. *listen to, analyze and describe music*

_____listen and move to show question and answer form

_____identify phrases as "question" or "answer"

7. *evaluate music and music performances*

_____justify/evaluate choice of instruments or movements for question and answer phrases

8. *understand relationships between music and other arts and disciplines*

_____relate musical question and answer phrases to questions and answers in conversation (language arts)

_____relate musical question and answer phrases to pictures in children's books (visual arts)

_____relate the words of a song to nature/life experiences (social studies)

_____use objects/streamers to show question and answer phrases (dance, visual arts)

9. *understand music in relation to history and culture*

_____listen and respond to music intended to tell a story or express something in life experience (program music)

# Additional Activities

### Track 19    Here Is the Bee Hive

England

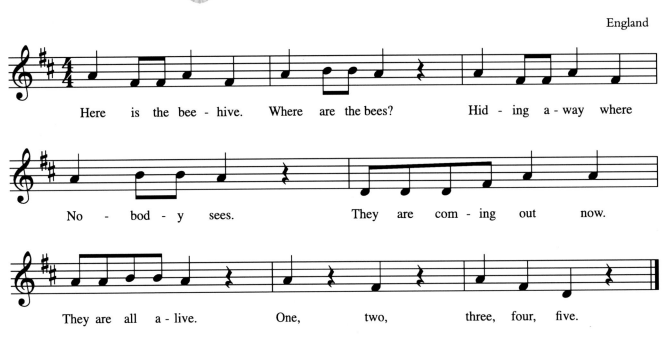

Here is the bee - hive. Where are the bees? Hid - ing a - way where

No - bod - y sees. They are com - ing out now.

They are all a - live. One, two, three, four, five.

### Track 20    Baa, Baa, Black Sheep

Traditional

Baa, baa black sheep, have you an - y wool? Yes, sir, yes, sir, three bags full.

One for the mas - ter, one for the dame, One for the lit - tle boy who lives in the lane.

Baa, baa, black sheep, have you an - y wool? Yes, sir, yes, sir, three bags full.

# Chapter 5: Rests in Music

At some point in our lives, most of us have had the experience of watching and waiting while an envelope is opened and an award winner is announced. For a few moments, the room is silent and a sense of drama and anticipation fills the air.

In a similar manner, musicians use silence to create a sense of drama and anticipation. The activities in Chapter 5 invite young learners to experience and explore the use of *rests* in music. Through guided exploration and experience, children discover that:

*Music may have rests (silences). Rests can be expressive.*

## The Puppy Takes a Rest

I know a secret about a puppy in our neighborhood. Would you like to know the secret? The puppy does something very interesting. When he is ready to take a rest, he stops running and barking—he makes no sound at all—and his ears begin to droop like this (place your thumbs by your ears and droop your fingers forward).

Sometimes, music takes a rest, too. Listen carefully. Can you hear the rests in this song?

**Track 21**    **Bow Wow Wow**

## Respond to a Story

**Focus**   *Sing and move to show rests in a song (standards 1 and 6).*

- Tell the story "The Puppy Takes a Rest."
- Sing or play the recording of "Bow Wow Wow."
- Repeat the song, inviting children to join in and use their hands to "droop their ears" during the rests.

*Note: Initially, children are invited to perform movements during the rests. With practice and experience, children grow in their ability to hear and respond to rests internally, without the support of physical movement.*

## Find the Rests

**Focus**   *Sing and move to show rests (standards 1 and 6).*

*Identify silence as a "rest" (standard 6).*

- Say: "Watch and listen. Raise your hand if you see a place where my hands pat the beat, but my voice takes a rest."
- Sing "Bow Wow Wow." Pat your lap and pause dramatically during the rests.
- Ask: "Did you see a place where my hands pat, but my voice took a rest?" (yes)
- "This time, let's sing "Bow Wow Wow" and pat the beat on our laps. Show the rests with your hands." (turn palms upward during the rests)

## Create New Movements

**Focus**   *Create new movements to show rests (standard 4).*

*Evaluate/justify movement choices (standard 7).*

- Say: "Let's sing 'Bow Wow Wow' and pat the beat on our laps." "Be sure to show the rests with your hands." (turn palms upward during the rests)
- Ask: "Can you think of another way to show the rests?" (touch shoulders, touch mouth, touch ears)
- Assist children in making appropriate choices. "Does this movement show a rest?" "Could we make a movement without sound?"
- Sing the song again, incorporating the children's ideas.

## Sing in Question and Answer

**Focus**   *Sing and move to show rests (standards 1 and 6).*

*Sing in question and answer form (standard 1).*

- Divide children into two groups.
- Ask Group one to sing the question phrase.
- Ask Group two to sing the answer phrase.
- "Don't forget to pat the beat and let your hands 'rest' when the song takes a rest." (turn palms upward)

## Play a *Singing Game*

**Focus**    *Play a singing game (standard 1).*

- Sing "Bow Wow Wow."
- Demonstrate the movements as you sing.
- Encourage children to sing and move with you.

| *Words* | *Movement* |
|---------|------------|
| Bow wow wow, | Step three times in place. |
| Whose dog art thou? | Shake index finger (as if scolding). |
| Little Tommy Tucker's dog. | Turn around in a circle. |
| Bow wow wow. | Clap three times. |
| Woof! | Jump in the air. |

## Play a *Statue Game*

**Focus**    *Listen and improvise body shapes during rests (standards 3 and 6).*

**Materials**    *Hand drum and mallet*

- Invite children to find a "personal space" within the room.
- Say: "Listen to the drum. Step with the drum. Stop and make a 'shape like a statue' when the drum takes a rest."
- Tap a steady beat on the drum.
- Challenge children to stop (as quickly as possible) when the drum takes a rest.

# Pease Porridge Hot

England

Pease Porridge hot!
Pease Porridge cold!
Pease Porridge in the pot,
Nine days old!
Some like it hot!
Some like it cold!
Some like it in the pot,
Nine days old!

## Learn a New Rhyme

**Focus**    *Identify a silence as a "rest" (standard 6).*

*Listen and move to show rests in a rhyme (standards 1 and 6).*

Track 22

- Pat the beat and say the rhyme, "Pease Porridge Hot."
- Ask: "Is there a place where my hands pat, but my voice takes a rest?" (yes) "Is there another place?" (yes)
- Ask: "Can you pat the beat and show the rests?" (turn palms upward during the rests)
- Say the rhyme slowly, allowing time for children to show the rests.
- Repeat the rhyme, encouraging children to say the words with you.

## Create Rest Movements

**Focus**    *Create movements for rests (standards 1 and 6).*

- Review "Pease Porridge Hot."
- Say: "Today, let's create special movements for the rests."
- Guide children to create movements to perform during the rests. Ask leading questions: "How shall we show that the porridge is cold?" "How shall we show that the porridge is hot?" "How shall we show that the porridge is old?"
- Say the rhyme together, incorporating the suggested movements during the rests.

*Note: children may enjoy adding sounds with their movements.*

## "Read" Rests

**Focus**    *Relate rests in music to pictures (standard 8).*

*Perform rests in response to pictures (standard 5).*

**Materials**    *Copy masters 5-A and 5-B (pictures)*

- Place four pictures (the fourth picture is blank) on the board.
- Say: "What do you see in the pictures?"
- Ask: "Which picture is a rest?" "Why do you think so?"
- Say: "Let's say the words as I point to the pictures."
- Say: "Now, cover your eyes while I rearrange the pictures."
- Challenge children to 'pat and say' the new pattern (turn palms upward during the rest).

Track 23 **Naughty Kitty Cat**

Hungary

Naugh - ty    kit - ty    cat,        Why    did    you    do    that?

You  have  but - ter    on    your  whisk - ers,    Naugh - ty    kit - ty    cat!    Scat!

*Verse 1*
Naughty kitty cat,
Why did you do that?
You have butter on your whiskers,
Naughty kitty cat.
Scat!

*Movement*
Shake finger as if scolding.
Shake finger as if scolding.
Stroke long whiskers on face.
Shake finger as if scolding.
Throw fingers outward.

*Verse 2*
Pretty kitty cat,
Sitting on your mat.
No more butter on your whiskers,
Pretty kitty cat.
Meow!

Stroke hair.
Sit down.
Stroke long whiskers on face.
Stroke hair.
Throw fingers outward.

## Learn a New Song

**Focus**  *Sing a song that includes rests (standard 1).*

- Say: "Listen to the words of this song. Do you think the cat is in trouble?"
  "Why do you think so?"

- Sing or play the recording of "Naughty Kitty Cat."
- Invite responses from the children.
- Say: "Let's pretend to be Mrs. MacDonald and shake our fingers at the cat."
- Sing the song slowly, modeling the movements.

## Sing in Question and Answer

**Focus**    *Sing "Naughty Kitty Cat" in question and answer form (standard 1).*

- Divide the children into two groups.
- Ask Group one to sing the question phrase of "Naughty Kitty Cat."
- Ask Group two to sing the answer phrase.
- If children are successful, switch parts.

## Read Picture Strips

**Focus**    *Perform rests in response to pictures (standards 1 and 5).*

*Create new movements for rests (standard 4).*

*Evaluate/justify movement choices (standard 7).*

**Materials**  *Copy masters 5-C and 5-D (cats)*

- Place four picture strips on the board.
- Say: "Let's pat the beat and sing 'Naughty Kitty Cat.'"
- Touch the pictures as the children sing.
- Ask: "Why are some pictures different?" "Shall we pat our laps during the rests?"
- Suggest: "Let's try a different movement during the rests." (e.g., turn palms upward, touch shoulders, touch lips)

## Play Instruments

**Focus**    *Perform rests in response to pictures (standards 2 and 5).*

*Evaluate/justify performance choices (standard 7).*

**Materials**  *Copy masters 5-C and 5-D (cats)*

*Rhythm sticks*

- Distribute rhythm sticks.
- Say: "Let's sing 'Naughty Kitty Cat' and tap our sticks."
- Point to the picture strips as the children tap (one tap per picture).
- Ask: "Should we tap our rhythm sticks during the rests?" "Why or why not?"
- Ask: "How shall we show the rests with the instruments?"

## Puppet Patterns

**Focus** *Arrange puppets to show rests (standard 4).*

*Identify ways to "write" rests with puppets (standard 5).*

**Materials** *Four puppets or stuffed toys with one-syllable names (e.g., cat, dog, frog, pig).*

- Choose four children to hold the puppets and stand in a row in front of the group.
- Challenge the group to pat the beat and say the names of the puppets (from left to right).
- Ask: "How can we show a rest?" (turn the puppet around, turn the child around, hide the item behind the child's back).
- Choose one of the puppets to be a "rest."
- Ask: "What will we do when we see a rest?"
- Say: "Let's 'pat and say' the new pattern!"
- If the children perform successfully, choose different puppets to be "rests."

## "Royal March of the Lion"
## Carnival of the Animals

Camille Saint-Saëns
(France, 1835–1921)

### Who Am I?

I am a special cat. I like to lie down and sleep. Sometimes I sleep 20 hours a day. I have gold-colored eyes that can see very well in the dark. I like to hunt at night. Sometimes I walk 5 miles a day. I am big and powerful and proud. I have a loud roar. Some people call me the "King of Beasts." Do you know who I am?

## What Do Lions Do?

**Focus**   *Discuss/reflect on the lifestyle of a lion.*

**Materials**   *Copy master 5-E (lion)*

- Read "Who Am I?"
- Show a picture of a lion (copy master 5-E).
- Ask: "What do lions do?"
- Encourage children to think beyond "roar" and "hunt."
- (Ideas: sleep, yawn, stretch, blink eyes, wiggle ears, walk, stop, listen, look around, eat, drink, rub against a tree, twitch tail.)

## Pretend to be a Lion

**Focus**   *Relate rests to nature/life experiences (standard 8).*

*Experience the lifestyle of a lion through creative drama (standard 8).*

- Invite children to find a personal space in the room.
- When they are ready, remind them that they are welcome to make their own movements and sounds, but they must be careful not to bump or distract anyone else.
- Read the following statements, one at a time.
- Allow time between each statement for the children to perform the actions.

*"Pretend that you are a lion. Sit down and imagine you are asleep."*
*"Wake up and open your eyes."*
*"Stretch and yawn."*
*"Stand up slowly."*
*"Look around......look up....look down."*
*"Freeze and listen!"*
*"Blink your eyes."*
*"Wiggle your ears."*
*"Walk like a king."*
*"Stop and roar."*
*"Eat some food."*
*"Drink some water."*
*"Rub against a tree."*
*"Twitch your tail."*
*"Walk back to your sleeping place."*
*"Sit down and fall asleep."*
*"Wake up—you are yourself again!"*

### Listen and Imagine

**Focus** *Listen and identify a rest (standard 6).*

*Relate a rest in music to nature (standard 8).*

*Identify the meaning and purpose of rests in music intended to tell a story or express something in life experience (standard 9).*

- Say: "In a moment, I am going to play the "Royal March of the Lion." There is a special rest in this music—a long rest called a 'grand pause.' Listen and raise your hand when you hear the grand pause."

**Track 24**
- Play the "Royal March of the Lion."
- Say: "Close your eyes (or put your head down) and imagine the lion. It is early morning and the sun is rising on the African plain."
- Ask: "What do you think the lion is doing in this music?" "What do you think the lion is doing during the rest?" "How does the lion walk?" "How does the lion move during the roar?"
- Play the "Royal March of the Lion."
- Encourage individuals to discuss and demonstrate their ideas.

### Play a *Mirror Game*

**Focus** *Listen and move to show a rest in music (standard 6).*

*Relate a rest in music to nature (standard 8).*

- Say: "Today, let's imagine that it is early morning on an African plain. The lions are asleep. The sun is just coming up."

**Track 24**
- Say: "Watch and be my mirror."
- Play the "Royal March of the Lion."
- Demonstrate the movements as the music plays.

| Approximate time in the recording | Action |
|---|---|
| .00 seconds | Wake up. Open eyes, roll shoulders. Stretch, yawn. |
| .30 seconds | Freeze and listen. |
| .33 seconds | Look around proudly. |
| .45 seconds | Walk hands on lap. |
| 1.05 minutes | Raise hands up and roar (4 times). |
| 1.25 minutes | Walk hands on lap. |
| 1.50 minutes | One last big roar. |
| 1.55 minutes | Fall asleep. |

*Approximate length of music: 2 minutes*

## Move Freely with the Music

**Focus**  *Listen and respond to program music composed in 19th century France (standards 6 and 9).*

- When children are familiar with the "Royal March of the Lion," provide an opportunity for free response.
- Say: "Today, you may move as you like. Listen to the music." "Move the way the music sounds" or "Let the music tell you how to move."
- Say: "Let's begin by finding a space in the room." "Lie down and pretend to be asleep."

**Track 24**
- Play the "Royal March of the Lion."

# Let's Review!

As the year progresses, continue to reinforce new learning in music.

### Ideas

1. As new songs and rhymes are introduced, listen for rests (e.g., "Two Little Blackbirds," "Little Sally Walker," Kindergarten Book 2).
2. Create a soft accompaniment for a song.
3. Choose instruments to play a steady beat for a singing game.
4. Draw pictures for the questions and answers in a song.
5. Think of a way to demonstrate beat, soft and loud, tempo, question and answer, and rests—using one song.

# How Are We Doing?

## Rests in Music

Are individuals able to:

1. *sing, alone and with others, a varied repertoire*

____sing a song that includes rests

____say a rhyme that includes rests

2. *perform, alone and with others, on instruments*

____perform and show rests with instruments

3. *improvise*

____improvise movements or body shapes during rests

4. *compose and arrange*

____choose/create rest movements

____create movements or sounds for rests in rhymes or songs

____arrange pictures/puppets to show rests

5. *read and notate*

____perform rests in response to pictures/icons

____identify ways to "write" rests with pictures or puppets

6. *listen to, analyze and describe music*

____listen and move to show rests

____identify/define silence as a "rest"

____listen and identify rests

7. *evaluate music and music performances*

____evaluate/justify performance choices for rests

8. *understand relationships between music and other arts and disciplines*

____relate rests in music to pictures (visual art)

____relate rests in music to nature/life experiences (language/social studies/nature)

9. *understand music in relation to history and culture*

____identify the meaning and purpose of rests in music intended to tell a story or express something in life experience (program music)

____listen and respond to program music composed in 19th century France

# Additional Activities

### Track 25    Sally Go 'Round the Sun

Traditional

**Formation**

Circle with players facing the center.

**Action**

A sun, a moon, and a chimney pot are placed on the floor within the circle. Players step around an object and back to place as each name is sung (Johnny go 'round the sun, Carrie go 'round the moon, Jenny go 'round the chimney pot, etc.). Everyone jumps in place during the word "boom." The game is played until everyone has had a chance to walk around an object.

### Track 26    Jolly Old Saint Nicholas

Traditional

# Copy Master 1–A

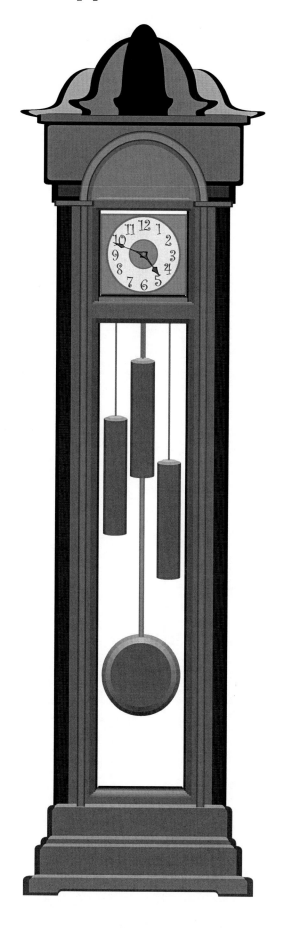

# Copy Master 1–B

# Copy Master 1–B

# Copy Master 1–C

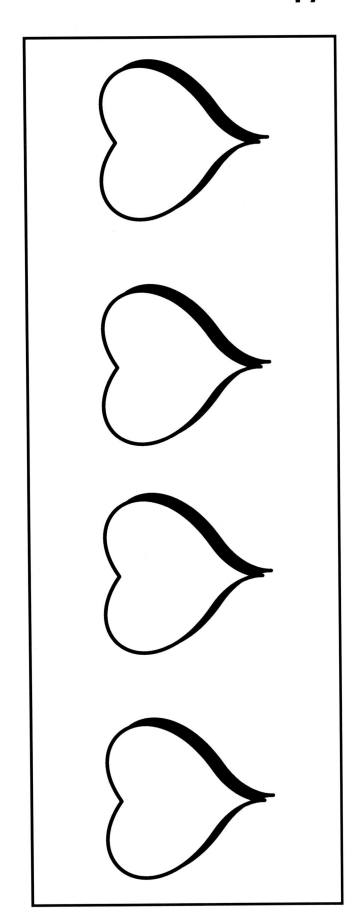

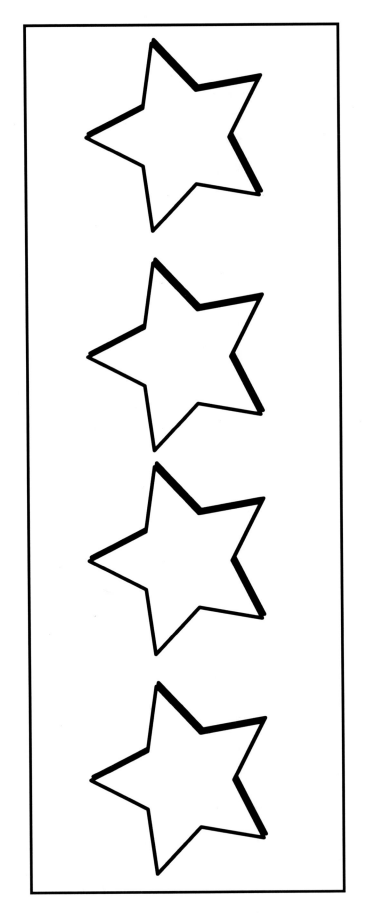

# Copy Master 2–A

# Copy Master 2–B

# Copy Master 2–C

# Copy Master 2–D

# Copy Master 2–E

# Copy Master 2–F

# Copy Master 2–G

# Copy Master 3–A

# Copy Master 4–A

# Copy Master 4–B

# Copy Master 4–C

# Copy Master 4–D

# Copy Master 5–A

# Copy Master 5–B

# Copy Master 5–C

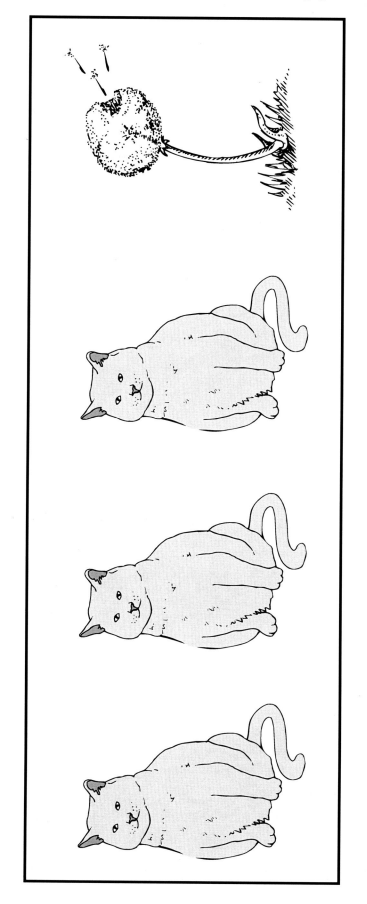

# Copy Master 5–D

# Copy Master 5–E

# Index of Music and Rhymes

# CD Track List

| Track | Title |
|-------|-------|
| 1. | Johnny Works With One Hammer |
| 2. | Hickory Dickory Dock |
| 3. | Sousa's "The Stars and Stripes Forever" |
| 4. | Hickety Tickety Bumble Bee |
| 5. | Old MacDonald |
| 6. | Hush Little Baby |
| 7. | If You're Happy |
| 8. | Two Little Sausages |
| 9. | Haydn's "Surprise Symphony" |
| 10. | Five Little Pumpkins |
| 11. | Get On Board |
| 12. | Paige's Train |
| 13. | Engine, Engine |
| 14. | The Old Gray Cat |
| 15. | Doggie, Doggie |
| 16. | Here is the Bee Hive (chant) |
| 17. | All the Little Ducklings |
| 18. | Schumann's "The Wild Horseman" |
| 19. | Here is the Bee Hive (song) |
| 20. | Baa, Baa, Black Sheep |
| 21. | Bow Wow Wow |
| 22. | Pease Porridge Hot |
| 23. | Naughty Kitty Cat |
| 24. | Saint-Saëns' "Royal March of the Lion" |
| 25. | Sally Go 'Round the Sun |
| 26. | Jolly Old Saint Nicholas |

## CD Credits

**Orchestrations** by Momcat Studios except: Haydn's "Surprise Symphony," and Sousa's "The Stars and Stripes Forever," licensed from *Network Music.*

**Piano Performances** of Schumann's "The Wild Horseman" by Michael Dean, and Saint-Saëns' "Royal March of the Lion" by Michael Dean and Courtney J. Crappell.

## About the Author

 Dr. Joy Nelson directs the Kodály Programs at the University of Oklahoma, where she is the Samuel Roberts Noble Presidential Professor. Awarded the Oklahoma Regents' Award for Superior Teaching, she supervises student teachers and teaches graduate and undergraduate courses in music education. Before moving to the university level, she taught music in grades K-6 in the state of Washington and earned a Doctor of Musical Arts degree from Stanford University.

Joy is the author of numerous articles about music reading, listening, creative drama, puppetry, and curriculum planning. A popular clinician, she travels frequently to make presentations and give workshops for in-service teachers. She spends her summers directing and teaching seminars in the Kodály approach.

Joy lives in Oklahoma with her husband, a performing musician and retired professor, and enjoys gardening and trying new recipes.